How
a poe
dying

C000213166

How can you write a poem when you're dying of AIDS?

Edited by John Harold

CASSELL

Cassell
Villiers House, 41/47 Strand
London WC2N 5JE

387 Park Avenue South
New York, NY 10016-8810

First published 1993

British Library Cataloguing-in-Publication Data
A catalogue record for this book is available from the British Library.

ISBN 0 304 32904 5

Designed and typeset by Ronald Clark
Printed and bound in Great Britain by
Biddles Ltd, Guildford and King's Lynn

Contents

Foreword

Even as 'an outsider looking in', reading these poems I felt a very personal sense of loss. I also felt proud. Through their mature responses to the tragedy of HIV/AIDS, many homosexuals have gone beyond the coming-out; it's a coming of age. We are standing together as never before.

This anthology is a moving tribute to lives and loves; the fact that its sales will benefit the Lesbian and Gay Bereavement Project somehow completes the circle . . .

> 'I was afraid to die
>   But with friends like you I shall live forever.'

Pam St Clement

Preface

The poems contained in this collection were sent to me after I advertised in *Capital Gay* and *The Pink Paper* in July 1992.

Initially, I chose twenty-one poems from the massive amount I was sent. These twenty-one I decided to use as readings between the nine movements of a requiem mass I was in the process of writing. These poems are now, with one omission, the first you will read in this collection, with another thirty-two selected from the rest.

All the poems I received affected me in some way. Some made me cry. All made me think deeper about what it is to be living as a gay man in the shadow of AIDS.

These poems have a unique strength and dignity about them which reflect the writers. I am pleased and proud of the new friendships I have formed as a result of this project, all of which have helped me to understand a lot more of the feelings in the poems.

As I write, the requiem mass, *Undying Heart: A Requiem for AIDS,* is nearing the end of its rehearsals, and I am in the process of contacting celebrities to perform the poems and imbue them with the stature they deserve. Proceeds from the performances and from the sales of this book will go to the Lesbian and Gay Bereavement Project. Volunteers of this organization work tirelessly with those left behind after losing a loved one.

I look forward to welcoming you to future performances of the requiem, and hope that you gain as much from this book as I have.

John Harold
July 1993

Acknowledgments

Many thanks to Peter Tatchell for his invaluable help, and to Steve Cook and Roz Hopkins at Cassell for their support, encouragement, respect and faith. To Louis I am deeply indebted for helping me unscramble my thoughts and for always being there. My wonderful friends deserve a vote of thanks for their patience and for keeping my feet on the ground. My partner, Steve, was a tower of strength and great inspiration throughout my work on this anthology. I am grateful to Alistair Hulme and the Names Project (UK) based in Edinburgh (tel: 031 555 3446) for providing artwork for the cover.

Special gratitude is due to all the poets for allowing us to glimpse their pain, their hopes and their love.

J H

*These poems are dedicated to
those who have suffered and died,
those who are fighting and surviving, and
those who care and give so much.*

The Poems

How can you write a poem when you're dying of AIDS?

How can you write a poem when you're dying of AIDS,
When you have a reputation for maintaining poetic grades?
You write with clarity and elegance
And what you produce might just be flatulence.

The poem is too harsh – too incisive – too intrusive.
How can you write a poem when you're dying of AIDS?
I've read the schmaltz – the badly written – the desperate,
They cannot squeeze their tears onto the keyboards.

They hide as we all hide.
Being open we hide and being hidden we hide.
How can you write a poem when you're dying of AIDS?

I was beautiful.
Now in restaurants people stare at my disfigurements;
They are afraid.
I am afraid.
The good ones don't know what to say,
The bad ones run.

'But James how do you feel about dying?'
HOW THE FUCK DO YOU THINK I FEEL ABOUT DYING!
I am 35,
I had a potentially brilliant career ahead of me,
All my ambitions were lying in front of me
Waiting to be picked off like ducks in a gallery,
And I was a good shot.

[1]

How can you write a poem when you're dying of AIDS?
When the drugs in you fight to get the best side effects.
When the morphine makes you wander unaware and incontinent.
When the steroids in reducing your swellings make you swell.
When the painkillers give you headaches.

How can you write a poem when you're dying of AIDS?
When you crawl to your family – your brother – your sister.

I say 'I know you have to be ashamed of me,
I know your neighbours must never know
For if they did your loving friends might talk about you.
So I won't go on telly.
I did go on the radio but only so that you would never know.
I won't even appear in my home town in case a neighbour sees me.
(Though last year, sister, you wanted the neighbour to see
the big shiny Volvo I drove).'
I make all these concessions crawling on my knees because
I NEED YOUR LOVE.
You spit on me.

How can you write a poem when you're dying of AIDS?
Your real friends are helpless and hopeless.
They want to help but I haven't got the strength to tell
Them how.
They get depressed;
I get guilty.

How can you write a poem when you're dying of AIDS?
MY LOVER ALAN I CANNOT WRITE OF HIM.

How can you write a poem when you're dying of AIDS?
When you are such a burden to so many.
When you are such a worry to so many.
When you are such an embarrassment to so many.
When if you were an Englishman you'd take the honourable way
out.
I'm too scared for that.

How can you write a poem when you're dying of AIDS?
I can't . . . can you?

JAMES SYKES

[3]

On Sunday 24 January 1988, a candlelight procession took place in London in memory of those who had died in the UK from AIDS. The route started in Hyde Park and proceeded along Park Lane, Haymarket, Piccadilly, Trafalgar Square and along Whitehall past Downing Street into Parliament Square, where it finally stopped outside the Queen Elizabeth Conference Centre. As many as could of the 5000 present gathered in the square and observed a two-minute silence, then dispersed.

Memorare

The flickering light
unsteady in my glass
susceptible to each
new gust of wind,
constantly being re-lit
cradled against the capricious
breeze
reminded me of you.
The last ten months of your life.
Your loving life flamed fight
against AIDS.

Around me other candles
witnessed for the loved,
now dead.
The brave flames of those
with AIDS and HIV
borne unashamedly with
fierce joy.

[4]

And many more
Acolytes
Brothers and sisters
bonded
by this act of love,
this
Memorare.

In the silence
I cried.
Tear-sealed eyes
like a blind man
for whom light
can only be a memory.
Oh, my lovely light!
Where are you now?
extinguishing the hazarded
flame
cradled in my hands.

Was then a brother
placed his arms around my grief.
'Look up!' he said.
And there flickering
in my eyes
a thousand lights
held high by saints
who loved.

You are not
gone.
No darkening night
can ever snuff,
put out
your love's light.
Inside me burned a pride
at being there
The shared care of it.
And you,
shone brighter
in the gathering dusk.

M V LIVELY

It's murder

There are lies I ought to tell you of how I've fought and lost
a war but these fail to render beyond the tears of friends
who battled and have gone before. Old comrades
whose only bullet was the fear that someone else may suffer
the indignity of being a socialite for what time is left to be
a brother. People playing parts in a crusade that they
were neither conscripted or volunteered to, still victimless,
are losing all they have yet their last breath spares a thought
for you. And at the end of it all does anybody give a damn,
make a final grasp for sanity or is the agony of reality
too much to bear on the breast of some beleaguered profanity,
like an octophobic conscience, too scared to admit to reason
and lose its ideals, we carry on as before in our busy lives
not wanting to be aware of those whose fates are sealed.

WALTER MCINNES

The dilemmas of AIDS

It's AIDS and I don't know what to do.
I've had it for years and I don't know what to do.
It gets worse and I don't know what to do.
I've had more advice from more quarters than I knew existed
And I don't know what to do.
People come to me and they say,
When they are honest,
They don't know what to do.
They ask
What *can* I do to help?
What can *I* tell them?
Some of them want to make commando raids on my psyche
And reveal in moments that which I've not discovered myself.
If I can't do it, I'm not being positive enough.
Not cooperating.

The professional carers have trained voices unless you ask for money.

The hospitals want to help –
They have to help –
Every fibre of their being is programmed to help.
They come across an illness they can't help.
Then like mad robots
They prod
And poke
And test
And slice.
And many times
They kill.

These views are not the views of a cynic,
But after these years they are the views of the sceptic.

Long ago and far away I wrote:

> Blood freed from the trapped body
> Washed across the floors of pain
> And sank into the head
> Of the failed healer.
>
> The healer cried
> The body died
> The blood just tried
> To LIVE.

The worst of it is I understand why they all do this.
I understand.

But
I don't know what to do.

JAMES SYKES

Death is not The End

Death is not The End
But the beginning
Of a metamorphosis.
For matter is never destroyed
Only transformed
And rearranged –
Often more perfectly.
Witness how in the moment of the caterpillar's death
The beauty of the butterfly is born
And released from the prison of the cocoon
It flies free.

PETER TATCHELL

Death

Our bodies entwined in an image of love
Yet separate we lie, so close together
Our warmth sleeps in the hour of darkness.

I never cried before tonight.
The tears shed are words of love
So wasted now

As you lay here, still in my arms . . .

PHILIP WASLEY

Black leather jacket
for Johnny

My black leather jacket rubs and sticks,
hot and stubborn.
'You have to suffer for style.'
Your voice is wicked,
body like a stick insect,
in pyjamas with stripes,
saying 'hospital property'.

I hold your hand which is enormous
and want to fill the bed
with petals, silks, feathers to soften
the bones that tug at your skin
to run away.

The beard isn't you.

You don't smoke unfiltered Gauloises anymore.
The smell would rise from the garden
as you bent and planted and built
and trimmed and picked and
made so much from nothing.

Yesterday I bought flowers for you.
Marched them from Hyde Park to Trafalgar.
Wilting, rather ghastly dahlias
were all they had.

We were three thousand,
one for each who has died.
Men sobbed in Piccadilly
over white lilies,
hands tight on stems,
teeth sore.

You ask imperiously,
'Which is better, to be happy or to be right?'
I smile.
You would have scoffed at Louise Hay six months ago.
You look happy.
And haven't the wind to laugh.

'Go quickly now,' you order.
Your mouth moves like a butterfly under the mask.
'Take those yellow roses, all of them,
I've not enough room.'
Your eyes are as big as your heart,
bluer than the sky you can't see from the bed.

Your black leather jacket creaks as I kiss you.
It rubs and sticks, smells of sex and clubs and streets
and tells of firm hands that have stroked it,
rushed it off, to love you.
It is important to keep it on.

CHERRY SMYTH

[13]

For Kevin Bills

Friend
We gaze for you
who travels stars.
Light years, planets,
Universes;
Are the domain of your smile.

We, earthbound.
sigh at the lightness
of your going.

M V LIVELY

Wisdom, that granite virtue, will not budge

'Barry? Why, Barry's dead, man. Weren't you there
and praying for the first and only time?
"Give me his pain, I'm stronger!" Oh, you longed
to take his place, and couldn't. Now it's done.
His dad said you took care of everything,
you were a tower of strength. "I just don't know,"
his mum said, tearful (tears were denied to you),
"how we'd have coped without poor Barry's friend."
It's over. You must live what time you have,
a hard way and a long one faces you,
so make him your goodbyes, and take the road.'

> Rest then, darling happy one!
> Gloom and smiles alike are done;
> anger, patience; loss and gain;
> no delight now, nor no pain.
> All's now silence, numb repose
> and my wild love to bind you close.
> Deep oblivion be your friend –
> so my mourning has its end.

TED NORMAN

And the sun was shining brightly

There is a day when I shall die: when I shall wake to the sound of the radio, wash in tepid water, dress in yesterday's clothes, look at myself in the mirror . . .

The rituals of living are a prelude to death. I practise them everyday in preparation.

For even men who have decided that today they will die . . . look out of the window at the weather.

To that extent I commit suicide everyday, without ever actually killing myself.

HOWARD I LESTER

When all the visitors have gone

When all the visitors have gone
I think of you alone in this room
lying still.
Their heat and fume evaporates
The fading flowers of conversation
dying:
like the blooms on your locker.
They,
I,
Bus-tube entombed, scurry home
for fireside reassurance.

I thought of you
staring for emptiness.
The fitful waking dreams
in whose schemed skies
the death star first appears.
I thought of you alone.
Yet you alone
mind-numbed must reach to it
and taste its captured rapture.
This is so.

When every visitor has gone
the heat and fume dissipating
I'll think of you.
Mute conversations
lying still
in the flower faded air.
And there
weep softly
for love's living
transient bloom.

M V LIVELY

Icarus

We are as angels
falling to the sea.
Our graceless number
Icarus calls.
Fated,
life's tinselled
waxing wing
is the precursor
of our end.

We loving self,
(and the self in others)
high fliers
defied the sum
of man's ingratitude.
Bold arcs we made
deifying the setting sun.
Difference was our dare.
Revellers in the love of it.

We are as angels
falling to the sea.
Grounded with leaden wings
for Icarus calls
and the tears of the unloved
foretold this
finite night.

M V LIVELY

Time for . . .

It's funny that such a little word can have such a big effect
taking time for others, as well as for oneself,
just giving comfort at a time it is needed
a helping hand, when an arm is outstretched,
seeking guidance and stability.
Knowing the time to speak words of encouragement
and the times to keep silent – just to listen
having to offer one's shoulder, when needed,
giving something – expecting nothing in return.

Caring for others spontaneously, not having to think about it,
crossing that particular bridge, when one comes to the stream.
Time is the most precious gift one can offer others,
and the most important thing is – it's free.
It just needs giving to reap the rewards . . .

B J ALLEN

What now?

for Steve

Sitting alone again. Waiting.

You left an hour ago but it seems like weeks.
Already I feel lost inside, trying to decide
Just what to do.

A night of passion and lust
Of soft-spoken words that meant far too much
You did everything so right and I think that
I might
Be in love with you.

I promised myself this time would be new
I wouldn't fall in love so easily
But I can't seem to stop myself.

Being in love with you feels so right to me.

It happened purely by chance.
I'm glad you made the first move.

That's not my style.

Though from day two
You know I wanted you

(And now there's nothing I wouldn't do!)

[20]

It's hard to believe those feelings are back again.
It has taken me so long!
It's been so hard for me
To let myself go enough to feel that
This can't be wrong.

So
What now?

I don't want to fall too deeply, too quickly.

Hell! I don't even know where I stand!

I know where I want to be and
I hope you want the same from me . . .

JOHN YATES

By candlelight

The candle lights his eyes so bright,
They pull me into their depth and I can't hold back.
Flickering shadows dance through his spiky hair
And my heart dances with them.

I feel the warmth of his youthful flesh
And trace a delicate pattern on his chest.
Light fingertips – the softest touch,
His skin so smooth.

His breathing deepens – he sighs.
His beautiful chest rises and falls under my palm.
His hands reach for my shoulders
And I feel their warmth as he pulls me gently down.

Chest against chest, our hearts beat in time.
His face pressed close to mine – a trickling tear joins us together.

Tightly we embrace and hold our pose,
Neither willing to let go.
I could hold him forever.
The contentment, the happiness.

And now the tears flow – and he cries with me.
I trace the path of his tears with my thumbs as the candlelight
flickers in his misty eyes.

He smiles at me.
I shake my head in disbelief that this beauty can be mine.
His sensitive hands glide softly down my back, reaching low.
I shiver and close my eyes.

[22]

I move my lips to his, aware of every place our bodies touch.
His body heat, his carressing fingertips, his tender lips,
A kiss that never ends.

In turn we make our love.
The pain of his pleasure is exquisite,
My own pleasure seemingly endless – suspended in time.
The deepest fulfilment I have ever known.

As the candle burns lower he falls asleep in my arms.
I watch the shadows dance over his naked form.
I press my lips to his temple and realise I'm lost.
Lost in his beauty
And lost forever in his love.

STUART LEE GROOM

Love me like there's no tomorrow

Wrapped up tight in that well again
Where deep my hidden treasure lies
Haunted by those years gone by
Now intoxicated by your eyes

Could you soothe the silence of my soul
In this complex web I weave
Could you clear my misty skies
'Cos I'm aching to believe

That you could love me like there's no tomorrow
Find me whirling in your ocean of love
Bathe me captive, crush my pain and sorrow
While my heart greets the stars above

Am I hell-bent or heaven-bound?
Should I summon my reinforcements?
While I quiver on the verge of a miracle
In overdrive my mind spins around
Past memories flash as yearning torments

Thirsty heart wears too many scars
Guarded close by a cage of fear
I want to saturate the grey with blue
Quench the parched and love's ecstasy share

Then love me like there's no tomorrow
Find me whirling in your ocean of love
Bathe me captive, crush my pain and sorrow
While my heart greets the stars above

[24]

Yes! Love me like there's no tomorrow
Find me whirling in your ocean of love
Bathe me captive, crush my pain and sorrow
While my heart greets the stars above.

KEITH PARKE

Outside looking in

Close to my soul
Deep down inside
There lies the truth
That lies can't hide
And here I stand
Where hope has died
From the outside looking in.

Before the door
I stand in vain
And wait for words
That might explain
Why I'm alone?
Why all this pain?
From the outside looking in.

Behind the wall
That blocks my road
My senses scream
My dreams explode
I curse the juice
That never flowed
From the outside looking in.

What does it take to get over the rainbow
Over the fear and the doubt
How do you get from the place where you are –
To the space on the inside
Looking out?

My faith in me
Is not a dream
I like myself
So it would seem
I shall regain my self-esteem
From the inside looking out

And I will star
And I will fly
Become the earth
The moon, the sky
And I will know
The reasons why
From the inside looking out

Two simple words
Two words that say
I will survive beyond today
Who has the power to see me through?

I do   I do   I do   I do

KEITH PARKE

First dream of Chris

Last night you entered
into my dreams.
Almost casually
we were talking . . .
'Are you alright?'
I asked, scanning with
the dreamed eye
your familiar form.

I cannot remember your eyes –
It seemed as if you turned
away from me,
as you replied in a low voice;
'I will be better.'

Into my dreams
almost casually
I was talking to you
scanning with dreamed eyes
your familiar form.

M V LIVELY

Soft, for music dies

Soft, for music dies within this room.
Where once the bridge that Heaven sings
to man, returning him to grace
is empty space.
Soft, for music silenced never can return
and we the living, must
its passing mourn,
sighing in the gloom.

Soft, still within the silence, lies the love
he crafted here upon an earthly stave;
The song, moon slivered nights
and sunscaped days.
Soft, threading memory stakes the muted claim
which we the living,
tearful bear,
the blame denial of our grave.

Soft, dying music's timbre strikes the note
discordant; Chaos brings the age of truth.
To him returns all harmony
and places, times innocence.
Soft, here the living ache,
seek the dawn of melodies.
Each day his love reborn
sustains undying hopes.

M V LIVELY

Eternal love

We both knew it was time for you to go
and I, with dread, would face the emptiness,
the unremitting loneliness,
the unrelenting end.
Your eyes gave me that one last look
of love
and – so it seemed – of something more.
Its meaning I could not then comprehend.

And so you left I thought for good
but still that look remained.
And it was then I understood.
This was not to be the end at all.

Your body may have gone, it's true.
But bodies change from day to day,
new cells reborn as old decay
Not so that inner self that makes you you,
That changeless self lives on, lives through.

The love we share,
much stronger than mere memory that fades,
goes on and grows and floods back in cascades
And overwhelmed, my very being dissolves
to merge with yours again.

You're with me
when the dewdrops glisten at tomorrow's dawn.
You're with me
when the sun's rays lift the veil of misty morn.
You're with me
when the thrushes greet the day with song.
I feel you at my side the whole day long.

When shadows lengthen
You're still at my side.

And when night falls
and sleep takes rein,
you're there, once more,
close to my heart again.

JOHN LACORTE

The dreaming

Elation!
No truth!
It never happened!
It was a nightmare!
We can wake up now!

There is no sexually transmitted virus
There is no condemning finger pointing
There are no bodies suffering in the world
We can mix secretions without unknown secrets
We can celebrate our sexuality
    wherever, whenever, however and with whoever we want
We can experience the joys of the good old days
Man can love man can love woman can love woman
The only things being reclaimed will be rubber by industria and fetishists
Freddie is alive. Long live Queen.

Still – on we sleep . . .

GORDEN THOMAS-PURDY

A just cause

As you bite on the belt
of the freedom fighter
who struggles for what he loves
and gently chew on his heart
while he fondles his gun,
greasing the barrel which
might kill you.
Think not of the cause
for which you are about to die
in the same way that nobody else does.
Envelop him as you sink to
your knees in valiant defence, be
blown away only as those
who have lived can choose.
Fire on all cylinders
as you collapse into his arms
and take everything while you stand.
Writhe in the wake that
is to be yours, explode into
life and demand that
you leave your mark on mankind.
Believe then that you are
again in love as you are freed
with the wave of a caring hand.
Such power needs no cause
or battle to overcome, just
words and love from soldiers
in a battalion of one kind.

WALTER MCINNES

Hidden reflections

The look that says
Why oh why
Why me?
Why us?
Why now?
And so
The sun does shine outside
I share with you
Despair
For we do rain
So many tears
Within
Behind the mirror
and reflection
of ourselves
for only do we see
and only we
do recognise.

BRYAN SMITH

The kick inside

Friends don't know I'm dying.
Can I tell you?
Will you flee in fear?
Will you feel guilt?
Friends don't know I'm dying.

Help me please.
It's inside me.
I have no control over it!
Why me?
Help me please.

Friends don't know I'm dying.
I love you
You deserve to know!
How will we cope?
How will you cope?
How will I cope?
    Will we cope?

Friends don't know I'm dying.
Shall I just fade away?
I want so much to enjoy my life, to enjoy your life
I want to be remembered for the man I am
Nobody knows I'm dying.
    Do they need to?

GORDEN THOMAS-PURDY

Quietus est

I fell in love with him against my will. The silence of my desire laid me captive. I acquired a taste for despair, and shaved my head in penitence.

Then one night I made love to him. I held him still alive in my arms and, kissing him one last time, left him quiet in the morning sun.

*

Did you not tell me once that you desire your boyfriend most when he's asleep? You draw down the sheets and view his body, as pale as death's, in the half-light.

HOWARD I LESTER

From 74 to 90

When I had you
what did I acquire?

The skill to love?

The skill to laugh?

Inspiration to work?

Now, what do I have left?

My jungle?

My memory?

. . . my yellow teapot.

JANE BELLAMY

A day in the sun

So it was I vowed
in the angry adolescence
of my being
as I first sex-sniffed
the paper heroes
Spending my sperm
on the sheets
time and again . . .
'Bring me an hero
with burnished golden hair
steel blued, and eyes tempered
with the Hyacinth.
Put him on a dragon
all chrome and wheel.
Biking orgasmic dreams upon my hill . . .
Who'll empty me of all being.
Spurn with studded sulks
my affection's gaze.'
All this in my mind's haze
A day in the sun
enough . . . then Love is done.

How different
the middle-age experiment
proved.
Heroes came and went
Discontented sperm-knights
Spent. Spent.
Reaching in the primed pocket
for more change . . .
more change.
Love?
I was done.

Then in the inopportune
beer-clouded afternoon
My hero came.
Tall statured
with a quirkish,
fated grin,
dressed in irregular soldier's
dress.
The best of it –
he challenged . . .
'It would be a sin
not to buy me a lager!'

This was the cargo
on which we floated in,
Shared dreams and fantasies
Realised all.
Then
straddled bodies
sidled
for the embryonic curl.
Could this be love?
He/they/he thought.
Ought the Sun
be out?

The grass days
still dew your eyes.
Strength from your thighs
saps
for still being,
and I shoulder
the ragged umbrella
lest rain
raze out the sun.

Now is an age
of knowing
the deeper things.
And I become smaller;
for the eternal universe
rings our mortality . . .
The sun
begins to set.

So it was
I vowed
(in my adolescence) . . .
What exchange I promised
for this Sun-haze
I cannot remember
anyway . . .
All I can say . . .
You – I see
light fade.
Before the fallen night's
one brief respite
Whisper
for the breeze
'Thank you dear Chris'
this still,
this stillness . . .
is Love.

M V LIVELY

[40]

It's that time again

You've gone.

Already
(And for the millionth time)
I'm sitting in the chair where you sat;
I'm holding the pillow where you rested your head;
I'm sniffing the sheets where you shot your load;
I'm caressing the skin that you touched;
I'm folding and keeping the paper bag you left.

I treat everything you touch
like some sort of
Holy relic;
As if, by touching it,
some miracle will occur.

Some miracle does occur –
I come to life.

More so when I see you.

Already I'm wishing you were back here with me.

JOHN YATES

Good times, bad times, always

There will never be a good time
to tell a friend goodbye,
to help them take that extra pill
because there's nothing left to try.
There will never be a good time
to hold hands as life passes away,
to realise that you'll never again
kiss your lover at the end of the day.

I will care and love you though
    it breaks my heart to say goodbye.
We have loved each other beyond our time
    and I believe that one day I'll find
that the tears I now cry
    consecrate a love that cannot die.

There can never be a bad time
to tell someone that you really care,
to lose the fear of crying and
laying your emotions bare.
There can never be a bad time
to say that too many are going to die,
to hear that what I'm really trying to say
is 'I don't want to say goodbye'.

I will care and love you though
    it breaks my heart to say goodbye.
We have loved each other beyond our time
    and I believe that one day I'll find
that the tears I now cry
    consecrate a love that cannot die.

There will always be time
to tell how wonderful you'll forever be,
to look the world straight in the eye
and proclaim 'That was the man for me'.
There will always be time
to continue the fight you started,
to stop the suffering without reason
and save another's love from being parted.

I will care and love you though
    it breaks my heart to say goodbye.
We have loved each other beyond our time
    and I believe that one day I'll find
that the tears I now cry
    consecrate a love that cannot die.

WALTER MCINNES

The sickness unto death

Is it with such easy conscience that I perform my subtle acts
of murder? Dividing the world between the living and the dying;
exiling the sick, because their sickness discomforts me.

I am ashamed of the cruelty with which I lay claim to life.

Do the martyr-saints in Heaven, restored to health, crave
the freedom to die again? Are they captive of a munificent god?

If there is a land of the living and a land of the dead,
at least they lie within my domain. Between them is only
the difference of the choice I make.

HOWARD I LESTER

Grief

You told us that the souls of lovers twine.
I laughed. But my boyfriend thought it plain;
And told me so
    (I did not laugh again)
        and went his way
Alone.

I know his soul is feeding on me still,
Diseased and, wearied by disease, degraded.
And mine
    (Of that there was nothing much to tell)
        is rotting
On his bones.

I'm not a slave to conscience, nor care
That you despise me for not seeming brave.
To be alone
    (His kisses tempt me there)
        counterfeits his death
With sorrow.

HOWARD I LESTER

[45]

Unrealities

Still wandering about
lost in the haze,
Everyday living things puzzle me.
Nothing seems permanent.
Unsettled
body, mind refuses to
concentrate.

Up and down
on the emotional helter-skelter
I ride.
Down. Down.
Up. Up.
Like the glittering Sun
after storm clouds,
I smile for flowers,
But the bud of our love
feels stratified,
locked–ungreened
by your going.

Like a blind man
I search for you
in the morning fog.
Crying out for holding.
(How I would dance for
your body's warmth)
But here earthbound stay.

The glass of reality,
sees things as they really are.
Sees the nomad
lost in the haze
here–living.
And this earth's impermanence.

M V LIVELY

Ordinary people

Yesterday, we came to tell the world we're here
But the world we looked for wasn't there
So we took out a joint mortgage
On another planet, of lengthening shadows
By day, cosy silences
By night. All earthy modernity
Taken fright of two very ordinary people
Whose clothes, hair, ears, eyes
Would have taken no-one by surprise
But, rather, we'd have liked to hear it said
By more faces in glad places
While there was still time

See those two? They're friends of mine.

We tried to pretend it didn't matter
Because we had each other; but now
You're gone, dear friend. I stand alone
Against the tide of bitter sympathy
That threatens, just as it
Always did, you and I, for all
That we were two very ordinary people
Braving the same mud, sky
As any other pair in love
So twists of wire
That heap our grave
Conspire to show

See him? His friend was gay, you know.

R N TABER

[48]

Equality?

So you died my love.
There is no title for me
Should a wife lose her man
She's a widow
Stranger still
To her a pension is given.
Yet nothing for me
Why?
Ours was the love that's forbidden.

DAVID BROWN

Resurrection

I drop my eyes into a flowery pool
see the veins of one gay cheek
split, bare a thread
of ash light

against cold Stone trickles
a crimson grief
on angry fingers
fall hot tears

by chance alone, a friendly breeze
has spilled this, Nature's blood
not so a rebel heart
tearing, crushed

petals like confetti on the ground
our bodies whimpering without
sound, seeds scattered
in the wind

among the wreaths
a rose laid low
yet as I make
to go

risen again, newly crowned!
no glad petals to shine
but looks familiar
embracing mine

one by one, the letters
of your name break off
the stone, prick
the pool

this the moment, this the Peace
you and I together
making ripples
forever

Amen

R N TABER

Pain

Sometimes one feels anger and hurt
anger from within and the hurt for those gone
Other times one just feels lost
wandering aimlessly along . . .

Smiling and laughing then suddenly
remembering the reality, tears flow endlessly
Feelings of guilt are overwhelming
one should be glad they suffer no more pain . . .

But life isn't as clear cut as this
the loss one senses is enormous
Trying to cope with day to day tasks
drains what little energy one has left . . .

Focusing on what they used to look like
is difficult when looking at the little bundle
Perhaps tomorrow it will be more bearable
but tomorrow is a long time coming . . .

My friend, tomorrow does eventually arrive
you can visualise how they were before
That is the way you will remember them
for that is the way they want to be remembered . . .

B J ALLEN

Silent grief

When one's friend, that special friend,
passes on their journey home
one's world is torn apart – walls crumble –
one questions life about life
simple things seem so complex
easy tasks take on an enormous weight . . .

It is a traumatic experience at the best of times
but makes it ten fold when one can't talk
to be able to share the pain one feels
because it is a hidden grief that one can't
tell others about – one has to suffer in silence . . .

But one must air one's sadness to overcome
silence only makes pain more unbearable
your friend wouldn't want this measure of pain – not for you!
for your friend is still by your side, to help you,
to guide you as they have done for a lifetime
the only difference is you can't see them
but they walk beside you as always . . .

So be comforted by this and as time goes by
your own self will shine again
the one that they loved you for . . .
remember the times that you shared
and the warmth that the friendship gave to both
smile within from the fond memories that you both cherished
and be thankful that your lives crossed
for both were richer for it and the world a poorer place without . . .

B J ALLEN

[53]

Leaving

Sometimes one makes it onto the platform
to wave off family or friends
tears streaming down while the train pulls
out for the long journey homeward bound
remembering all the good times one shared
as well as some of the bad . . .

Sometimes one doesn't make it in time
to wave off family or friends
but one still feels the same emotions
and more – of guilt!
for not having the chance to say all
the things you wanted to say
before the train pulled away . . .

My friend, do not burden yourself unduly
for it was your loved one's way of saving
you the pain, hurt and distress of seeing
them off on the train homeward bound
for they knew what you wanted to say . . .

Cry and be sad a while but be comforted
that they will be home soon and one time
in the future you will be with them again
within that mansion in the sky
until that time they want you to live again
find that heartbeat that they loved
and meet life full on . . .

For as the sun rises in the morning – so shall you
for just as the sun sets in the evening – so shall you
they will be there, at the station, when your train
pulls in, to greet you . . .

B J ALLEN

Hologram

Your death has etched
an Hologram
within
in
and upon me.

So any trick of light
the beams which rest
on people's smiles,
the peeping eyed daffodils
of Spring
Throw its relief
sharp . . .
within
in
my very bones.

Even as I sleep
the Hologram of your death
dapples upon my outstretched hand
clutching for the embryo curl.
For you are
within
in
and diffused
in my dreams.

So our mortalities
are aligned.
The green light
of my existence
forever
signed
by death's Hologram.

M V LIVELY

The blanket of my love

As soon as you walked in tonight
I knew you'd been crying.
I saw that look in your eyes which said
'Please love me.'
Now is the only time
When I can reach out to you.
Only now,
when you're feeling so low.

It's now,
When you're so weak and helpless
That I can love you the most.
I know when you need my love;
Now. At these moments.
I'll always be there to give it to you.

I'd like to know I can love you
Without you crying.
I'd like to see that look in your eyes
All the time.
I'd like to know
I can always comfort you
And stop you
From feeling so low.

So come on and let go!
Fall into my arms. I'll hold you!
And I promise never to let you go.
I'll keep you safely by me
And stop the hurt inside you.
And wrap you in the blanket of my love.

JOHN YATES

The first move . . . and the best

Death holds my hand
and pulls me to the edge of the cliff.
Down there is my happiness
But I don't want to make the first move.
He smiles, reluctantly at first,
Before he pulls me over.

I want to scream
But nothing sticks in my empty throat
Nothing.
Nothing exists anymore
but the sound of the wind holding me up
and pushing me down.

I have been tricked, Death,
You have tricked me
and I'm glad.

I always knew I'd find true happiness here.
Down amongst the lost and lonely, the sad.

Why didn't I make the first move?

I'm better off now than I ever was.

JOHN YATES

The sensual world

I was afraid to die
But now I have, we can laugh at it all.
There is a time for pain
And a time to mourn
But I know that time will pass
And your lives will soldier on . . .

I'm on the other side of the looking-glass now
I can watch the world take place
My friends and lovers are more beautiful to me now than
    ever before.
The tides ebb and flow so quickly
Yet I can still see the flicker of remembrance in your faces
The marches you march on,
The politicians, public and officials you outrage,
The cures you search for,
The rights of life, dignity and welfare you fight for.
I am there in your hearts and memories, pushing you on
If not for me – for yourselves and others like you

I was afraid to die
    But with friends like you I shall live forever.

GORDEN THOMAS-PURDY

Another time and place

Tell me now
what do you see
beyond your far
and wildest dreams
Beyond the seas
Beyond the skies
And further than
The universe
Another place
Another time
Another Birth
Another Life
And no more death
For what you see
and you desire
your wish so shall
Come true
For heaven
Shall be your body's
Final command.

Wherever you so wish
To go or be
From then until
Eternity.

BRYAN SMITH

Body positive

Life, death!

Floods me, goads me
Leads me beside hot beaches
Where I run, a dazzling sea
Cheering me on; and I wonder
Where the lark has gone
That fixed me with its cheer
Before abandoning me here
Like a forgotten toy
Filled with the joy of its
Having played me out
Before going about
Nature's own
Business

Life, death!

Calls me, galls me
Urges me back, back to you
But we are gone, the taste of us
Honey on my tongue
Where we romped and played
Like tots in make-believe
Heading barefoot among jellyfish
For the Punch and Judy man
Who'll make us laugh
If anyone can
Before the sun goes down
And our time
Forgotten

[62]

Life, death!

Overtaken us now, beckoning
I'll not rush my pace, for
We already ran our race, won
A place among these stars
Enchanting this lulling swell
All's well; one lost toy recovered
And taken home, Punch and Judy
In a packing case sleeping it off
At some Bed and Breakfast
I, filled with such a night
Far exquisite for words
like those we shared
Before AIDS

R N TABER

[63]

Once more, dear friend

Death, rippling the summer corn
Like the stirrings of a child
Unborn, wondering in the womb
What freedom between cage and tomb?
So, I lift my head to a gorgeous sky
Loose a few more dreams, watch them fly
Like the tail of a child's kite
Flapping bravely against all heaven's might
Now, barely a flicker, waved out of sight
With tearful eye and puckered brow
The child I was, resuming now
Across wintry years to wet an eye
That otherwise might have stayed dry
In the summer air, seeking where it never found
Hurting without a sound
Feasting on the harvest corn
Fretting for all love unborn
Caged in a breast deprived of rest
Tired of hearing all's for the best
Weary of waiting for waiting's end
Lonely for want of a dear friend
Sailing on the summer corn, *free*
Smiling wistfully at me
Who's left with a heavy heart
To weather the pain that's let us part
Wounded by your look which says
Our world should have been a better place

Music, murmuring a summer breeze
Like a guitar strummed with artist's ease
To lull earth's restless womb
Before the breaking of The Storm
That's spreading alarm
Among the corn.
I spot a field mouse, or maybe not
So tiny, quick, soon forgot
And I should hasten my own tread
The music bursting in my head
O love, life! Instead
I'll linger in this summer place
And to the wind I'll lift the face
Of one who's glad he came to see
The passing of our history
Into such natural beauty
As I'd forgot is no less a part of me
Than these shoes badly worn
Through a world sadly torn
In two, three, more
By love, hate, war
Famine too I have to say
As in the corn I kneel to pray
To what or whom I may never know
But, dear friend, I cannot let you go
Without thanks for this day
That's let me stay

R N TABER

[65]

A tape of Chris playing his music on an unknown piano

Remember . . .
all the folklore, myth,
romanticism.
The method.
Fingering technique
Major Minor chords.
Pedals
and decay.
Sustain.
Stave lines.
All that perplexing business
of the pianoforte . . .
you were going to show me
one day.

Dream-gleamed piano
you would play . . .
I saw it steaming
like a polished panther
in the garden room.
Ivory teeth
ready to devour demure pupils.
I would have polished it with
beeswaxed caution,
In breath-held fascination
one day . . . one day.
One day the money would be found.

Last night,
I found a tape
of you playing an unknown piano.
A yellow-eyed cat you teased,
tweaking your compositions
on his tail . . . his growl
was most satisfactory.
His eyes
now sunfilled lazy sostenuto . . .
then
flicking green-lifed allegros
with a hiss
he'd gone.

You whispering Vivace!
in his ears.

M V LIVELY

On bereavement

The sea, the sea
Reminisces me
Its shapes, sounds, swell
The two of us playing
Children in the sand
Making waves, marking well
Sunshine in the hair, each`
Teasing limb keeping time
With the ice-cream man

The sea, the sea
Braves me
Its shapes, sounds, swell
The two of us lying
Lovers in the sand
Making waves, marking well
Each nuance of flesh
Consuming us, and
Gulls cry

The sea, the sea
You, me
Shapes, sounds, swell
Children in the sand
Making waves, lovers
Resuming now and then
Our castles in the air
Marking a time for us
Eternity, to share

R N TABER

[68]

4 U

You are to me
that idyllic hilltop house
with countless rooms
each filled with a different new thing
always more magical than the last secret

that one huge solitary rock
to which I anchor the ship
of my very existence
whilst surrounded by stormy seas
ceaselessly threatening to engulf me

that sword of truth
shining like the brightest, tiniest diamond
on the black velvetness of my life
quietly illuminating with its strength
all that it touches

that one childhood happiness
amplified and eternal
always remembered and cherished
fondly and with warmth
of absolute affection

that adventure of a lifetime
the long-awaited, longed-for holiday
an exploration of the new and
familiar territory
I've always loved.

You are to me
like coming home.

JOHN YATES

A bright light still shines

Sometimes I feel the pain ain't gonna end
Sometimes I feel my heart might never mend
A lake of buried tears hidden in my secret place
And I can't hide what shows upon my face

Yet after all this time
When you read between the lines
A bright light still shines.

The wealth of my soul lies patiently in wait
It carries more hope than I could ever state
I'm learning to love . . . there's no joy in hate
And I'm so thrilled with my dreams of late

Yes after all this time
When you read between the lines
A bright light still shines.

Early abuse that carries such a cost
I hold on tight to a child I thought I'd lost
A frail sparrow with broken wings
Tender love and his heart sings.

And after all this time
When you read between the lines
A bright light still shines

I won't try to get even . . . I'll learn how to get close
No use in me tearing up . . . what I need the most
I need so to share and I won't conceal
The scars deep inside the pain that I feel.

Still after all this time
When you read between the lines
A bright light still shines

And after all this time
When you read between the lines
A bright light still shines.

KEITH PARKE

Endless life

Life's like a bird in endless flight
And through the universe it flies
Onto a hand past darkened skies
Rotating slowly day and night
And guided by a pale moonlight.

Where seas shall separate the land
Where mountains form from grains of sand
And trees and flowers and pastures green
where chosen children few have seen.

With rivers deep and mountains high
A paradise for you and I
For every time my heart shall beat
So does the earth beneath my feet.

More valuable than gifts of gold
A gift of life for we behold
So when you see a bird in flight
When life seems cruel and seldom bright
Reach to the skies and then fly too
Pass mountains high to seas of blue
To trees and flowers and pastures green
Where chosen children few have been.

BRYAN SMITH

Love, Dolly

How thoughtful that you have considered
Someone who even though being thoughtful
yet fails by way of frailty from accomplishing
simple tasks such as thank-you gifts.

Energy has gone, consumerism a foregone abstinence,
Another going without, fail to collect the basic
staples, fizzy pop a luxury not yet secured,
Confidence only in the passing, lazy idle tiredness.

The undertow swirling away stability,
Reason why the asking is still hard,
Steadfast and single-minded taking isn't easy.

Articulating gratitude, imparting the subliminal
accumulative of the it, that it,
We share as a two-way street.

Thank you friend for tolerance and words unsaid.
Thank you friend for being in my sight,
the just being there even when absent.

Thank you for remaining available
supportive and unjudgemental.
Thank you not just for me, but for what we are.

Love, Dolly.

TERENCE WILLIAM COOKE (A.K.A. DOLLY)

[73]

The light of home

I feel your wonder around me
Like a cloud in a storm
The thunder and lightning
Your love lights up my life

I hold your memory to me
So warm and secure
The pain I have in me
Alone to endure

None can remove it
Your love in my heart
Forever it is with me
Though we are apart

Tenderly I reach out for
Those memories of mine
Times that seem so far off
Of moments divine

And though I am alone now
You will always be near
And when I'm feeling lonely
It's your voice that I hear

One day, that's not far off
Together we will roam
In a place I'm yet unsure of
A paradise we'll call home.

DAVID BROWN

Index of authors

Notes on contributors

Bryan John Allen, b. 1954, lives in Newcastle.

Jane Bellamy, b. 1957, lives in Plymouth.

David Brown, b. 1955, lives in Middlesex. The inspiration behind his poems, written in Ibiza 1992, was his partner, Michael, who died in June 1989.

Terence William Cooke (a.k.a. Dolly), b. 1954, died in Amsterdam on 20 July 1992. His poem was written as a thank-you to his buddies, helpers and friends for their kindness during the worst of his illness. It was submitted to the editor by Dolly's friend, Tom Galloway.

Stuart Lee Groom, b. 1964, lives in Kent.

John Lacorte, born in Malta, lives in Dorset and sings with the London Gay Mens Choir.

Howard I Lester, b. 1964, lives in London.

M V Lively, b. 1943, lives in Leytonstone. Other work has appeared in *Catholic AIDS Link* magazine.

Walter McInnes, b. 1962, lives in Dundee.

Ted Norman, b. 1925, founder of the London Gay Mens Choir, died on 24 June 1993.

Keith Parke, b. 1955, lives in London.

Bryan Smith, b. 1964, lives in London.

Cherry Smyth, born in Ireland, works in London as a journalist and author. Her poem, *Black leather jacket*, is dedicated to Johnny Sheppard, and first appeared in *Of Eros and Dust* (Oscars Press, 1992).

James Sykes, b. 1953, died at the London Lighthouse on 6 June 1989. Poems submitted by his friend, Henry

Robertson, and published by kind permission of James' partner, Alan Campbell.

Roger Noel Taber, b. 1945, lives in London.

Peter Tatchell, b. 1953 in Australia, lives in London.

Gorden Thomas-Purdy, b. 1966 in New Zealand, sings with the London Gay Mens Choir and lives in London.

Philip Wasley, b. 1963, lives in London.

John Yates (a.k.a. John Harold), b. 1966, is the editor of this anthology and the composer of *Undying Heart: A Requiem for AIDS*. He lives in Leytonstone.